THE SOLE GIVER

THIS BOOK IS A HEARTFELT TRIBUTE TO THOSE WHO SELFLESSLY GIVE MORE THAN THEY RECEIVE—THROUGH SMALL YET MEANINGFUL ACTS OF KINDNESS, DRIVEN BY THE PURE JOY OF BRINGING A SMILE TO SOMEONE ELSE'S FACE.

PEARSON JOSEPH FERNANDES

Made with ❤ on the Notion Press Platform
www.notionpress.com

For my readers, who breathe life into these pages.

For those who give alot only to see others smile, even if it's just for a while.

It's just worth the watch.

I know you feel this too , so this book is dedicated for you.

Contents

Preface — vii

Acknowledgements — ix

Prologue — xi

1. Emotions Over Reality — 1

2. The Selfless Giver — 2

3. Everyone Over You — 3

4. Find Me In You. — 4

5. Served Ourselves Last — 6

6. The Gift Of Becoming Less — 7

7. Uncounted Acts Of Love — 8

8. The Giver Remains — 9

9. Soft Hands, Steady Spine — 10

10. Half A Prayer, Fully Meant — 11

11. In The Smallest Ways — 12

12. No Receipt For This Kind — 13

13. Joy In The Offering — 14

14. Kindness Without Cameras — 15

15. The Quiet Carriers — 16

16. The Ones Who Stayed — 17

17. Whole, Even When Empty — 18

18. Where We Chose To Stay — 19

19. The Warmth That Lingered — 20

20. Not Ours To Keep — 21

21. What We Chose To Hold — 22

Contents

22. Without Witness — 23

23. Through The Quiet — 24

24. What Remains Unsaid — 25

25. The Hands That Reached — 26

26. Small Things, Big Heart — 27

27. The Thread Between — 28

28. When We Were The Light — 29

29. Because We Could — 30

30. We Were The Quiet Kind — 31

31. The Softest Answer — 32

32. What We Left Behind — 33

33. More Than Enough — 34

34. The Ones Who Made Room — 35

35. The Gentle Way — 36

36. The Ones Who Didn't Leave — 37

37. Never Owed, Always Offered — 38

38. If No One Ever Knew — 39

39. For The Ones Who Understood — 40

40. The Sole Giver — 41

Afterword — 43

Preface

This book wasn't planned. It was felt.

It came together slowly—like how soft things tend to—between long nights, small conversations, and moments where I was giving more than I had words for.

The Sole Giver is for the ones who show up without being asked.

For the ones who pour without being poured into.

For those who love without measuring what's returned.

These poems are stitched from silence and kindness. They don't demand to be heard, but they deserve to be felt. If you've ever been the one holding the weight for someone else, the one carrying things quietly, this book was made for you.

You are not alone in your giving. You never were.

And through these words, I hope you feel seen—maybe even held.

— Pearson Joseph Fernandes

Acknowledgements

To every giver who kept going—even when no one noticed—this book is born from your spirit.

To my readers, thank you for holding these words, for reading between the lines, and for feeling the weight of the quiet love I tried to write about.

To the people who poured into me when I had nothing left to give—your kindness is stitched into every page.

To my family, my close loved ones, and my friends—thank you for your constant encouragement, your understanding silence, and the space you gave me to grow.

To those who challenged me, who taught me pain, patience, and depth—thank you for being part of the story, even if you never knew your role.

And to poetry for being the one place I could say everything, without having to say it all.

Prologue

Hey there. It's me—the kid who grew up just like everyone else. From being just a boy to a young, "irresponsible" one (that's what they say, right?). My journey's been a topsy-turvy ride, like it is for most men who's feelings feel tucked in, like socks in drawers no one opens. But it's time. Time we break the ice. Time we open up. How much does it really take to ask for a conversation? A quiet cup of tea? A walk by the sea? Or just to sit down right here, right now? Because I'll tell you everything. The when. The why. The how. But just a heads-up—hey, you might want to settle down, because your heart's going to melt down.

1. Emotions over reality

The world is a big place to live in,
But our emotions are the small world that we
live within.
We choose people over us for none that choose us.
Emotions over reality,
These words aren't for the wealthy,
You lived under dark clouds where the rainbow was never seen,
You've Lived in places where others have never been.
This isn't my last but my very first
I know these words will quench your thirst
So let's begin this endless ride
where emotions weigh more over pride.

2. The Selfless Giver

They lean on you in times of need,
Frame you with words that often mislead.
Yet as the day fades into the night,
It's you who stays, their guiding light.
True giving asks for no return,
But fills the heart with joy unearned.
For one who gives with love so pure,
Blessings will find you for this is sure
And though the world may fail to see,
The strength you give so selflessly,
Know that kindness leaves its trace,
Etched in hearts, a silent grace.

3. Everyone over you

You chose to love everyone but you,
for that's how the world shaped you too,
A two rupee coin in your pocket
for you spent it on somebody
cause your heart is like a diamond in the locket,
You relate to their emotions
when yours remain unseen,
"Stop being a mother to everyone,"
They say, almost routine.
But little did they know
The world is full of hands that take
yet only few will break
the silence to give, like you.

4. Find me in you.

You will look for me
in everyone who passes by,
You will know I was true
while the rest chose to lie.
Even the waves hushed
when you held my hand
That walk on the beach
felt like a vow unplanned.
You laughed like the sea,
wild and free,
But your heart held storms
you never let me see.
I gave you my calm,
you gave me your tide,
Now I drown in the thoughts
you chose to hide.
The sunsets still whisper
the shape of your name,
But they burn a bit colder
it's never the same.
I wait where we stood,
with sand in my shoes,

A lover you lost,
a love you'll reuse.
So if you feel stillness
in moments you knew,
Know I never left,
I'm just there in you.
In echoes and memories
you never outgrew...
You don't need to search,
you know where I grew.

5. Served Ourselves Last

We passed the plate
Full of the best parts of us,
We filled their cups while keeping ours dry,
We Said, "Take your time"
While the clock bruised our sky.
We laughed so they'd forget the storm
But we don't let them know where our tears come from
We dimmed so their light wouldn't flicker
held them strong even when we felt weaker.
We gave it all,
Not to be seen but with open hands.
Not out of lack but love that stands,
It's not a spell that one can cast
keeping them first,
we served ourselves last.

6. The Gift of Becoming Less

Sometimes the gift of becoming less isn't about losing,
It's about love that keeps the heart moving.
To love is a piece of art, the kind that shapes a soft heart.
The silence inside but the heart chose to volunteer outside.
The choice of loving people in disguise,
A quiet effort, Not seeking any prize.
It's never about being more or being less,
It's always about choosing love even if it's put you in distress
So we gave
not to vanish, but to uplift,
Wrapped all our love in a small gift
The world may never guess,
There's grace in the gift of becoming less.

7. Uncounted Acts of Love

Never kept a list,
Not of the nights I stayed awake,
The calls I've answered,
The fights I've ended without a word.
Even when it costs much I'd never ask anything back
Because love is the quiet kind with just fingeprints with no track.
You wont find me in the headlines
or stories that people shout out loud.
These are uncounted acts of love,
Not meant for praise or a crowd.
For I'd never wished for you to know but if i ever get the
opppurtunity
I'd definetly show.

8. The Giver Remains

Not built for the applause, Nor for Gain
Love is never meausred by what we obtain,
When laughter leaves the room
It's the silence that appears but the giver remains.
When you feel steady,
When you shoul'dnt be , look closely!
There should be a giver that works quietly.
And long after all the gratefulness runs dry
and the world forgets their names
The love will still linger around
while the Giver remains.

9. Soft Hands, Steady Spine

It isn't weakness,
When you love too deep,
Give freely and do broadcast
for let your silence speak.
Soft hands , Steady spine
That's how this phrase makes this poem taste like fine wine.
Yes you are reading this, It's you!
You are not waiting for any medals
or any signs,
Nor someone to lift you,
or draw the lines.
So if no one has told you
let this poem be your cue,
You're steady, you're soft,
You're powerful too.

10. Half a Prayer, Fully Meant

We didn't always know the words to say,
So we whispered hope in a clumsy way.
Not quite a hymn, not quite a chant
Just heartbeats stitched with what we meant.
We folded hands when no one saw,
Offered love without a clause or law.
It wasn't perfect, but it was real.
And still, the light found its way through,
In every small and sacred view.
The way we stayed, the way we bent
Half a prayer, yet fully meant.

11. In the Smallest Ways

It wasn't grand, it didn't shine,
No banners hung, no perfect line.
But there it was, a quiet grace.
A little light in an unseen place.
We just stayed close, we stayed near.
Love was shown through ordinary days,
In silent steps, in the smallest ways.
We gave with hands that asked for none,
Kept pouring out, though ours felt done.
Not for the glory or the praise
But because love lives in the smallest ways.

12. No Receipt for This Kind

There's no bill for the kindness they serve.
We gave more than what they deserve.
We gave like rivers give the rain,
Without a thought of loss or gain.
Not every love leaves marks or signs,
Some pass like wind between the pines.
We never asked for what's returned,
Just warmed the world where no one burned.
We stayed behind when all moved on,
Still showing up, still holding strong.
Not in the lights, but in the shade,
That's where real love's often made.
We knew that giving has no end,
But still we gave heart, time, and mind,
And left no receipt for this kind.

13. Joy in the Offering

We didn't give to fill a page,
Or carve our names in stone with age.
We gave because our hearts were full,
Not chasing praise, just feeling whole.
There's light that comes from giving free,
A peace that settles quietly.
No trumpet sound, no grand unveiling.
Just joy in the offering, never failing.
And if they ask what made us stay, When thanks were few and
skies turned gray.
We'll smile and say, "It wasn't tough," Love was the reason. That
was enough.

14. Kindness Without Cameras

No spotlight caught the things we did,
No record of the done good deeds.
We showed up soft, without a sound,
Where broken pieces could be found.
No crowd to cheer, no eyes to see,
But still we moved so faithfully.
It wasn't for the world to claim.
We gave, and never signed our name.
We weren't the story, we weren't the page,
But still we stood through quiet age.
Not out of duty, not for praise,
But simply born to love that way.

15. The Quiet Carriers

They held the weight without a sound,
Lifted others while staying down.
No need for banners, none for praise,
Just quiet hearts that chose to stay.
They patched the cracks with unseen thread,
Carried hopes that others shed.
You wouldn't know by how they move,
But they've walked miles in others' shoes.
They didn't speak of what they gave,
They built a life, they chose to brave.
And though the world may not recall.
The quiet carriers held it all.

16. The Ones Who Stayed

We didn't chase the brightest flame,
We didn't need the world to know our name.
We stayed when leaving looked like ease,
Planted roots beneath shaking trees.
We held the ground through storm and sway,
Chose to give, and not just pray.
Ours weren't the loudest hands in the room.
But they were the ones who still cleared gloom.
No medals hung for what we gave,
No stories carved above our grave.
But love was left in every trace.
In silent strength, we took our place.
Not for glory, not for fame—
But just to be the ones who stayed.

17. Whole, Even When Empty

We poured from places we never showed,
offering quiet warmth when we ourselves were cold.
We gave without knowing what would remain,
and still found meaning in the ache.
Some days, we were full of silence.
but even then, we never let anyone go unheard.
They saw calm on the outside,
but never the chaos we carried inside.
We walked away with empty hands,
but hearts still heavy with love unspent.
And maybe no one ever noticed,
but somehow,
we still felt whole.
Even when empty.

18. Where We Chose to Stay

We weren't the ones who walked away.
We stayed—when the silence got louder,
when the room felt colder,
when the reasons to leave outnumbered the reasons to stay.
We stayed through long pauses,
unfinished thoughts,
doors half closed.
Not out of duty.
but because love,
when real,
knows how to wait.
We didn't need a reason.
We just needed heart.
And when the world spun fast,
we chose stillness.
We stayed.
We stayed.
Even when no one asked us to.

19. The Warmth That Lingered

It wasn't in the words we said,

they came and went like tides.

It wasn't in the plans we made,

they changed with the wind.

But the warmth we left behind...

that stayed.

It clung to the corners of rooms,

to the breath in quiet spaces,

to the way someone felt

a little softer after we left.

We weren't always noticed,

but we were felt.

And long after the moment was gone,

our presence stayed behind,

like sun

on skin

you forgot was there.

20. Not Ours to Keep

We offered pieces
never meant to be held.
We gave comfort
without claiming a place,
left love
in places that didn't ask for it.
in people
who didn't know what to do with it.
It wasn't ours to keep.
And still,
we gave it fully.
We watched it leave,
sometimes quietly,
sometimes in pieces.
But we never regretted
what we handed over.
Because when love is real,
it never belongs to you,
it just passes through
and blesses whatever it touches.

21. What We Chose to Hold

There was no applause.
No spotlight.
No camera roll to rewind later.
But we were there
in the background,
in the shadows,
in the stillness between chaos.
We did things
that no one will ever know.
And still,
we did them with our whole heart.
Because some love
doesn't need a stage.
It needs presence.
It needs consistency.
Not everything that matters
makes a sound.
And the quietest acts
are often the ones
that carry the most weight.

22. Without Witness

There was no stage,
no waiting eyes,
Only moments
that made us rise.
The world moved on,
but we were there,
Love without witness,
offered with care.
What mattered most
was never seen,
But lived in everything
between.
A thousand moments,
a million steps.
Unseen, but still
the soul accepts.

23. Through the Quiet

We walked where silence had a name,
Not chasing light, not seeking fame.
We stayed behind when others flew,
And stitched the sky in softer blue.
No need to shout or stand out tall,
We caught what slipped, we broke the fall.
With gentle steps, we built a way,
That carried others day by day.
Not every truth is loud or bright,
Some only shine without the light.
And though our voices won't be loud,
We're always somewhere in the crowd.
So if you've felt a calm unknown,
It might have come from seeds we'd sown.
We've always walked beside, not through,
That's just what quiet hearts will do.

24. What Remains Unsaid

We didn't need to speak it out,
Some love is quiet—never loud.
It lives in looks, in pauses kept,
In nights we stayed while others slept.
It wasn't dressed in perfect lines,
But rested deep between the signs.
A hand held once, a breath held tight.
The kind of love that hides from light.
We never asked for it to show,
We simply felt it start to grow.
Not every bond is sharp or clear,
Some only bloom when no one's near.
And even now, without a sound,
It lingers still, it holds its ground.
For all the words we left unread,
The truest love remains unsaid.

25. The Hands That Reached

Before the fall,
before the cry,
Our hands were there,
we didn't ask why.
We reached through storms,
through fear, through doubt,
When no one came,
we still reached out.
It wasn't for praise
or tales retold,
But just because
our hearts were bold.
We didn't wait
for them to plead.
we reached out first
in time of need.

26. Small Things, Big Heart

A note left folded,
a door held wide,
A whispered word
when someone cried.
No golden crowns,
no stars to chart
Just quiet signs
of a giving heart.
We didn't need
to prove our grace,
We left it glowing
in every space.
For love's not loud,
but it leaves its mark.
In small things done
with a big, full heart.

27. The Thread Between

28. When We Were the Light

When hope felt thin
and nights ran long,
We showed up quietly,
held on strong.
Not to be heroes,
not to be right,
But just to be
someone's light.
And in that glow,
so dim, so bright.
We were the stars
in someone's night.
No need to shine
in every view.
We lit the way
for just a few.

29. Because We Could

*We stepped in slow,
no claim, no crown,
Just picked things up
when they fell down.
No trumpet sound,
no big reveal.
Just simple acts
with something real.
We helped because
it felt like truth,
Not out of debt,
or pride, or proof.
So if they ask
what made us move?
We did it just
because we could.*

30. We Were the Quiet Kind

We weren't the loudest
in the room,
But still we softened
every gloom.
We didn't push,
we didn't plead,
We simply showed up
where there was need.
No need to shout,
no call for fame.
We carried love
without a name.
And if you felt
a calm unwind,
That's how you knew
we were the quiet kind.

31. The Softest Answer

When anger rose,
we stayed the same,
A gentle word
instead of blame.
We didn't match
the world's sharp tone,
We gave it warmth,
we stood alone.
Our strength was not
in clash or cry,
But in the way
we let storms pass by.
No fists, no fire,
no force, no stance
Just kindness,
as the softest answer's chance.

32. What We Left Behind

We didn't leave
with trophies won,
Or tell the tales
of what was done.
But in our trail
were softer things.
A look, a pause,
a breeze with wings.
The love we gave
won't shout or shine,
But lives in hearts
we touched in time.
And long after
we're off their mind.
They'll feel the weight
of what we left behind.

33. More Than Enough

We didn't dress
our love in gold,
But offered warmth
in quiet hold.
No perfect words,
no flawless plan.
Just open hearts
and willing hands.
We gave what little
we could find,
But filled the space
we left behind.
And though they never
asked for much
We gave them more.
we gave them us.

34. The Ones Who Made Room

We stepped aside
so they could grow,
Made space for seeds
we'd never sow.
We didn't shrink,
we didn't fade.
But honored what
their light displayed.
We cleared the way
so they could bloom,
Became the ones
who made the room.
And even if
they never knew,
We found our joy
in letting through.

35. The Gentle Way

*We didn't need
to win the fight,
We only wanted
to do what's right.
No need to raise
a sharper voice,
We made the calm
our kind of choice.
The world was loud,
but we stayed still,
With gentle words
and steady will.
In the end,
we mattered more,
because we stayed
kind at the core.*

36. The Ones Who Didn't Leave

We stayed behind
when doors were shut,
Sat in silence
when words were cut.
We stayed through storms,
through aching skies,
With tired hearts
and open eyes.
Not bound by promise,
just by grace,
The kind that holds
in any place.
So when they say
who really grieved.
Remember us,
the ones who didn't leave.

37. Never Owed, Always Offered

*No one owed us
what we gave,
It wasn't debt
we sought to save.
We did not wait
to be repaid,
Or track the cost
of what we laid.
We simply shared,
because we could,
Not for the thanks,
but for the good.
And even when
they walked away,
We'd still give
again today.*

38. If No One Ever Knew

*If no one knew
what we went through,
we'd still give love,
steady and true.
Not every gift
needs to be seen,
some grace is quiet,
soft, and clean.
We asked for nothing,
gave with ease,
found our truth
in silent peace.
And if it flew
without a name.
It still was love,
just not for fame.*

39. For the Ones Who Understood

We never had
to speak too loud,
We weren't the type
to draw a crowd.
But in our silence,
there was grace,
A knowing heart,
a softer place.
We saw the cracks
they tried to hide,
And stood there
quietly by their side.
This one's for those
who simply knew,
Without a word,
we made it through.

40. The Sole Giver

We loved without
a binding thread,
Poured from places
we never said.
We bent so others
wouldn't break,
We stayed awake
for someone's sake.
We gave,
not for a claim or crown,
But just to lift
what had fallen down.
And if they ask
who bore the flame?
It was the Sole Giver.
Without name.

Afterword

If you've reached here,

you've walked through soft footsteps,

unseen moments,

and the hearts of those

who chose others over themselves.

This book was never meant to be loud.

It was meant to sit beside you quietly.

like the kind of love that doesn't need to be declared

to be deeply known.

To the givers,

the silent holders,

the ones who bend so others don't break,

you are not forgotten.

Your love doesn't disappear

just because no one saw it.

It lives on in how the world still turns,

in how someone made it through a day

because you stayed.

The world may not always applaud

what is done without credit,

but poetry does.

And now,

so does this book.

—Pearson Joseph Fernandes